Ethical Pitfalls for Professional Organizers

Debbie Stanley

Thoughts in Order

Austin, TX

Ethical Pitfalls for Professional Organizers

Thoughts In Order

www.ThoughtsInOrder.com

ISBNs:

1st print edition (2008): 9780985276812

1st digital edition (2019): 9780985276843 (epub), 9780985276850 (mobi)

Front cover photo © Scot Spencer 2005. Used with permission.

Design reviewer: Kevi Chapman, Cat Graphics, Grosse Pointe Park, MI

Praise for *Ethical Pitfalls for Professional Organizers*

As our profession grows, ethics is becoming more important than ever. Deb Stanley presents startling insights that profoundly impact every professional organizer, new and veteran, in their daily interactions with clients and colleagues. This book will fast become the foundation of ethical thought for our industry. *Barry Izsak, CPO®; Past President, National Association of Productivity and Organizing Professionals, and author of* Organize Your Garage in No Time

A must-read for every professional organizer! In this groundbreaking book, Deb Stanley has masterfully taken on one of the most important issues confronting all professional organizers today. As a consistent advocate for industry ethics, she has collected solid principles, multiple scenarios, and references for further contemplation in a work that is sure to launch a renewed commitment to integrity in our rapidly growing industry. I have always believed that true leadership takes courage; here Deb has taken the first giant step. Let's keep the momentum going! *Sheila Delson, CPO-CD®; Past President and Certification Program Director, National Study Group on Chronic Disorganization (NSGCD, now Institute for Challenging Disorganization)*

There isn't a single topic of greater importance to our growing industry than ethics, and yet the topic has been barely addressed within our ranks to date. Deb Stanley does a terrific job explaining ethics, exploring ways we may encounter ethical challenges in our organizing work, and giving us tools to deal with such challenges when they arise. This extremely valuable book is timely and timeless. I encourage all professional organizers to read it and ruminate. *Porter Knight, CPO®, speaker, productivity trainer, and author of* Organized to Last: 5 Simple Steps to Staying Organized *(book/DVD)*

Also by Debbie Stanley

Books

The Organized Musician. Thoughts in Order, 2016

"Let Me Show You the Basement": A Guide to Staying Safe in Clients' Homes. Thoughts in Order, 2011

Newbie Pitfalls: 50 Obstacles on the Road to Success as a Professional Organizer and How to Avoid Them. Red Letter Day, 2004

Organize Your Home in No Time. Que, 2006

Organize Your Personal Finances in No Time. Que, 2005

NAPO-Curriculum Courses

OD1-101: Fundamental Organizing & Productivity Principles

OD4-402: Safety in the Organizing Environment

Find updates and new offerings at
www.ThoughtsInOrder.com

About the Author

Debbie Stanley is a licensed counselor, corporate psychologist, organization and productivity consultant, and owner of Thoughts In Order Counseling and Consulting, founded as Red Letter Day Professional Organizers in 1997. She holds a B.F.A. in journalism, M.A. in industrial and organizational psychology, and M.S. in mental health counseling.

Visit Debbie at www.ThoughtsInOrder.com.

Gratitude

Sincerest thanks go to Steve and Kyle for giving me the time to write, as always. Many thanks to my colleagues, especially Sheila Delson, Janice Gentles-Jones, Barry Izsak, Porter Knight, Eileen Koff, Judith Kolberg, Laurene Livesey-Park, Carrie Savage, my fellow NAPO-Michigan and NAPO-Austin Chapter members, attendees of my class "Demystifying Boundaries," and my peers and mentors in mental health services including my instructors and fellow learners with Capella University and fellow members of the Michigan Adolescent and Adult ADD Network for Professionals (MAAAN), all of whose input, encouragement, and inspiration aided the development of this book. Finally, thanks and admiration to all of my clients, who have given me the means and the motivation to learn.

TABLE OF CONTENTS

INTRODUCTION

Where I Got This Information, and Why It Matters

In developing this book, I studied ethical guidelines, teachings, and directives from fields known collectively as "helping professions"—primarily counseling, psychology, and social work—to extract guidance for professional organizers. I saw value in this for two reasons:

1. We often encounter mental health issues in our clients, so these professions offer the most direct route to guidance on working with such clients ethically.

2. These professions have been in existence longer than ours and they have identified, wrestled with, and set policy about many of the ethical pitfalls that ours, as a younger profession, is only beginning to recognize.

I believe professional organizing has the potential to evolve into a vocation that is recognized and respected as a credible helping profession (perhaps even one that is licensed), but for that to happen, we must shore up our understanding of and adherence to stringent ethical standards. At just over thirty years into its evolution, the organizing profession is seen by licensed mental health care providers as, at best, a viable paraprofessional (i.e. unlicensed) option for client or patient assistance and, at worst, an unregulated industry with myriad specializations and no cohesive or enforceable professional standards.

In order to join the ranks of the established helping professions, we must get our industry organized! We need to clearly define ourselves, in general and in all of our varied specialties, in a way that shows we know our boundaries and we understand our ethical obligation to remain within them. We have an important contribution to make, and other helping professionals are beginning to recognize that. More and more of them will trust us with referrals to their clients if they see that we can do our part without disrupting or impeding their work.

Why Can't We Just Use NAPO's or BCPO's Code of Ethics?

Members of the National Association of Productivity and Organizing Professionals (NAPO) have pledged to abide by the NAPO Code of Ethics, and so of course they should. The same is true of people who have earned the Certified Professional Organizer (CPO®) credential from the Board of Certification for Professional Organizers (BCPO): They have agreed to abide by the BCPO Code of Ethics, and they should.

These codes can't be faulted for their intentions, but they lack the comprehensiveness that many of us seek. They also lack guidance on the process of ethical decision-making; they tell us what to do but not why or how to do it. It can be difficult to translate the broad directives of these codes into rules of behavior for small, common, everyday scenarios—

the little gray areas that constitute the majority of ethical lapses.

As I began my course of study in mental health counseling and became immersed in the codes of ethics of the mental health professions, I found that I was able to see many more nuances in the NAPO Code of Ethics—possibilities that I would never have thought of without exposure to the more comprehensive codes I drew from in writing this book. I believe that you too will get more out of the NAPO and BCPO codes after you've considered the concepts and scenarios included here.

The NAPO and BCPO codes differ on the matter of enforcement. At this writing, NAPO's code is aspirational only—compliance is greatly hoped for, but there is no process for disciplining violators. BCPO's code is enforced among CPOs and prospective CPOs, but has no bearing on those who do not have this credential and do not intend to pursue it, thereby exempting a significant number of people in the profession.

Some NAPO members (a growing number of them, from my vantage point) have begun campaigning for NAPO to make its code enforceable, particularly since BCPO has set the precedent. If it did, NAPO would establish a significant commonality between itself and groups such as the American Counseling Association that grant membership to licensed helping professionals. Such an alignment would, in my opinion, increase the credibility of NAPO and its members with clients and professionals in other industries.

How to Use This Book

You can read it cover to cover, or you can dip in at any point. I've provided a keyword list at the end (replacing the print index for this digital edition), so you don't need to begin at the beginning to understand the terminology; just search for unfamiliar terms using your e-reader's search function and check the first usage of the term for a definition or explanation.

Chapter 1 introduces you to some foundational information about ethics, and Chapter 2 outlines eight key ethical tenets that will help to inform your interpretation of the potential pitfalls in the next chapter.

As you read the scenarios in Chapter 3, think about how you would handle them (resist dismissing them with the thought, "I would never get myself into a jam like that in the first place"!). These scenarios would also make for interesting peer-group discussion or role-playing. Try brainstorming with your colleagues to think of even more "sticky situations."

I recommend that you have an ethical dilemma in mind as you read Chapter 4, where you'll find a process for resolving ethical problems—and, by the way, notice the definition of a true ethical dilemma in Chapter 1. You might be surprised!

With Chapter 5 we get down to the stickiest of all sticky situations: Dealing with an unethical peer. Here's where the rubber meets the road in your ethical education. Finally, be sure to check out the References and Further Reading section for even more information.

When you've finished your first read, **please flag the decision-making model in Chapter 4 and keep this book handy.** If I can accomplish just one thing with this effort, I want it to be that professional organizers know how to make measured, well-considered, well-informed decisions about ethical questions. I believe the guidance I have gathered and relayed here will make that possible.

Hey, Are You Talking about Me?

The scenarios in Chapter 3 are inspired by a wide variety of sources: Experiences I've had, vignettes I've read in other books, stories people have told me, and my imagination. As I composed them, I actively avoided "telling tales out of school" and changed identifying details in those scenarios that are based on someone's true-life experience. I've included real-sounding names in some stories to give them an authentic feel, but I do not know, or know of, any actual persons by those names. If one of the vignettes sounds like something you saw/did/heard about/were the victim of, or if your name appears in an example, please know it's a coincidence.

A Note to the Future

Ethical engagement in research, including ethical treatment of research participants, is a significant topic in the helping professions. At this writing, the professional organizing industry conducts little to no original research, but it can be anticipated that in the future, research efforts involving clients and other human subjects will be undertaken. At that time it will become important to review the voluminous ethical guidance on this subject which is available for members of the helping professions.

CHAPTER 1: WHAT IS (OR ARE) ETHICS?

Before you even say it, it's confusing: Is "ethics" singular or plural? It can be either, depending on the usage. When we talk about the study of ethics, it's singular: "Ethics is an important topic." When we're discussing ethics as a collection of guidelines, the word is plural: "Ethics are discussed in detail in this book."

Ethics is often used interchangeably with other words that name ways of guiding people's conduct. Here are a few comparisons of what ethics is and isn't (or are and aren't):

- *Ethics are rules for conduct that serve to protect that which a particular group deems important.* They are generally based on moral principles derived from the broadest cultural standards of the people to whom they apply. A set of commonly referenced moral principles that support ethical thought are discussed in the next section.

- *Ethics are not values.* Values are an individual's beliefs about everyday living. They have wide variance from one person to the next. A person does not have to hold an ethic as one of their values to comply with it, but if their values conflict with the group's code of ethics to such an extent that they cannot abide by that code, they should resign from the group.

- *Ethics are not mores (pronounced "MORE-ays").* Mores are community standards for conduct. They are more regionally variable than ethics but less individually variable than values. An example is the tradition of people in southern Ohio who pull over, get out of the car, and stand respectfully by the side of the road to allow a funeral procession to pass. People will often mistake the mores of their community for global ethics (some Ohioans are surprised to learn that not every community shows such respect for the departed).

• *Ethics are not laws.* Ethics are not directly enforceable by legal means, although there can be serious consequences for violating them, including censure and expulsion from a professional group. Some laws are also ethics, which gives the illusion that ethical violators can be prosecuted, but not all ethics are laws. To make it even more interesting, can you think of a situation in which a behavior would be ethical but illegal?

• *Ethics is not professionalism.* It is possible to do something that is ethical yet unprofessional (such as failing to return calls in a timely manner) or unethical yet professional (such as some forms of high-pressure sales).

• *Ethics is not religion.* Many religions include teachings that parallel ethical tenets, so ethics is often familiar to and appreciated by people who practice a religion. However, it is not necessary to subscribe to any religion to benefit from or adhere to ethical thought.

• *Ethics is not a list of loopholes.* If your rationale for a decision was "NAPO doesn't say I can't," you might be on shaky ethical ground. "Emphasize not so much what is permitted as what is preferred" (Jordan & Meara, 1990, p. 112).

• *Ethics is not a witch hunt.* It's true that some people use codes of ethics to "seek and destroy" a colleague whom they perceive has harmed them. This is not how ethics is meant to be used: It engenders bullying in some and in others it causes a constraining fear of making mistakes or having their actions misinterpreted.

Six Moral Principles

The mental health literature cites a variety of moral principles upon which to build an ethical framework. Here are six that recur in my sources. In the absence of a formal code of ethics to follow, a person could build their own personal code with these or any other moral principles that they find meaningful.

1. **Autonomy:** This refers to clients' freedom to make their own choices. Forcing clients to discard items violates this principle.

2. **Nonmaleficence:** This means avoiding harm; refraining from actions that might hurt clients. Refraining from chastising a client for backsliding supports this principle.

3. **Beneficence**: This goes beyond avoiding harm to actively promoting good for others. Participating in charitable events during National Get Organized Month supports this principle.

9

4. **Justice:** This means demonstrating fairness through equal treatment. Setting your price based on the affluence of a client's zip code would be unjust.

5. **Fidelity:** This means being worthy of trust; keeping your promises. Everything from showing up on time to living up to your marketing messages supports this principle.

6. **Veracity:** Put simply, this means truthfulness. Being honest with clients about your level of experience supports this principle.

Dawn Is Breaking

Ethics has a reputation as a maddeningly gray area, and this is not entirely undeserved. However, it's a case of "don't shoot the messenger": ethics attempts to clarify matters that are close to hopelessly ambiguous.

Imagine looking down your street a few minutes before dawn: It's not pitch dark but there is very little light, and it's difficult to make out the buildings, cars, or landscape down the road. If you wait a few minutes, though, there will be more light and you'll be better able to see. It still won't be as clear as midday, but it will be slightly less . . . well, gray. So it is with ethics and ethical decision-making. In most cases, taking the time to apply structured thought to a question will bring some enlightenment, but even so it rarely produces a single bright, shining answer.

A True Ethical Dilemma

We all encounter ethical decisions to be made every day. However, a true ethical dilemma is relatively rare. An ethical dilemma happens when you have "two or more good reasons to make two or more reasonable decisions" (Burkemper, 2002, p. 203).

Suppose you know of a woman who lives alone and whose house is heavily cluttered, moderately unclean, and stacked to the ceilings with newspapers. She is elderly and a smoker. She doesn't show any signs of dementia, though, and she has no physical disabilities that make it dangerous for her to live on her own. The only real problem—and it's a big one—is that her home is a firetrap. You're torn between butting out (which supports the principle of autonomy) and contacting the authorities to intervene for her safety (which supports the principle of beneficence).

On one hand, you figure you should leave her in peace because if you don't, "they" will throw out all of her stuff and force her into a nursing home where she'll be miserable. On the other hand, if you don't speak up, she could be hurt or killed in a fire and the hoard in her home would endanger the rescue workers who come to her aid. So you're back where you started: Either way could be argued as a reasonable decision, with more than one reason to choose it. What will you do? Chapter 4, "A Process for Ethical Decision-making," gives you a comprehensive method for resolving ethical

11

dilemmas like this one and includes a sample application of the process using this fictional case.

Maybe-Bad and Definitely-Bad

Here is another way in which ethics is not clear-cut: **boundary crossings** vs. **boundary violations**. In these phrases, the boundary in question is an ethic. A boundary crossing is, in casual terms, something that might be bad, while a boundary violation is something that is definitely bad.

Because ethical decisions depend heavily on context, it is possible to make a choice that would be ethical in one situation but not in another. This often happens when people think of a new way of doing things and their innovation is not adequately addressed in the code of ethics they follow. Because they are in uncharted territory, working without the safety net of extensive ethical guidance, they are said to have performed a boundary crossing. In such situations, it is recommended that the person document especially carefully their reasons for making the choice, the anticipated benefit of crossing that boundary, and evidence of a thought process that ruled out any undue potential for harm.

Here's an example that might surprise you. Among many therapists, home visits—what professional organizers do routinely—are considered a boundary crossing because the predominant standard of care is to provide psychotherapy in the clinician's office or facility.

In contrast with a boundary crossing, a boundary violation is something that the ethical code forbids in any context, no matter how innovative or potentially helpful the practitioner might think it is. An example of a boundary violation in mental health is a therapist having sex with a client: No amount of rationalization or argument about therapeutic value can make this behavior acceptable. Ethical boundary violations are often also illegal.

OK, I'll Sweat the Small Stuff ... If I Can Spot It

True, the really big violations are pretty obvious. But what about those little things that you just never realized are unethical? This is easier to grasp if you think about someone else doing it.

Suppose you're at a NAPO chapter meeting and a new organizer says she's happy because her first client has given her first dibs on her discards. You can easily see the ethical pitfalls in this situation, but the other organizer is blissfully ignorant of them. THAT—that blissful ignorance—is what you're hoping to eliminate in yourself.

The answer is to review as many case studies as you can. Look for accounts of people making choices both ethical and unethical. You can read them in books or online, listen to them presented by your peers, or present your own as what-ifs to colleagues, friends, and yourself. You can draw them from daily headlines and from historical events that were both immediately, dramatically atrocious (9/11) and cumulatively, creepingly atrocious (the Holocaust). To keep from drowning in despair, please find some examples of good behavior too!

With the true stories, work backwards from the outcome and find or imagine how it might have started. What was it like for the person who ended up making this choice? How did they get from point A to point B? If the choice was a bad one, what flawed logic could have created this result? If it turned out to be an ethically defensible choice, what led the person to it? Was it difficult to stand up for what was right?

With the fictional case studies like those in Chapter 3 that give you the setup and end with the implied question "What would you do?," figure it out: What would you do? What other information would you need? Which of the moral principles are involved in the case? The process presented in Chapter 4 will help you with these speculative scenarios.

Studying in this way will allow you to build wisdom, and eventually you'll begin to make just-in-time connections between situations you've read and—look out!—the one you're about to step into. You'll hear the warning bells before you get your shoes dirty. Whew!

CHAPTER 2: KEY ETHICAL TENETS

This chapter discusses eight ethical tenets that are of particular relevance to the professional organizing industry. Client Dignity and Welfare appears first in recognition of its centrality in the codes of other helping professions: It is foundational to all of the others, including those which follow it here in alphabetical order.

You can think of these tenets as tools for decoding ethical problems. Like any other form of expertise, you will acquire more tools over time, but this basic kit will get you started and well on your way.

1. Client Dignity and Welfare

This is the broadest ethical tenet of all. It sets the stage for everything else. All of the codes of ethics that were reviewed for this book hold this as the highest ethical directive for the practitioners they address.

When upholding both of these values—client dignity and client welfare—you have a choice of two ways to do it. You can avoid actions that would undermine client dignity and welfare (the moral principle of nonmaleficence from Chapter 1) or you can perform actions that enhance them (beneficence). You don't have to be constantly beneficent to be ethical: No single person has the resources to do so. What is required is that you are always at least nonmaleficent: You do no harm.

The frightening thing here, and the reason it is the most important ethical tenet, is this: "Do no harm" is harder than it sounds. Harm can be something tangible like breaking a client's computer or installing a shelving system that falls and causes injury. It can also be intangible, such as hurting the client's feelings through insults, careless remarks, or even something as small as judgmental facial expressions. There are countless ways to harm a client in the course of our work, and many of them aren't obvious or even recognizable except in hindsight. Ethics is intended to help us see these pitfalls coming and dodge them, so that we can avoid doing harm, even inadvertently.

The Danger Zone of Diversity

"Diversity" is a blanket term referring to the many ways in which people are unique: race, ethnicity, nationality, and culture; gender, sex, and sexuality; religion and spirituality; age and developmental stage; education, intelligence, disability, access to opportunity, and socioeconomic status; even level of identification with societally imposed stereotypes, and many more. If you read those carefully and you aren't clear on what some of them even mean. . . well, I wasn't either when I started my master's in mental health counseling, and I was alarmed to realize that I had been working with clients for ten years with very little grasp of the vastness of diversity and the potential to do harm through ignorance.

Sociologists teach us that ethnocentrism (a preference for and comfort with people who look and act like us) and even cultural encapsulation (obliviousness to what life is like outside our own culture) are natural. We're born with these tendencies. However, in a progressive society, it behooves us to overcome them and it falls to those of the majority or non-oppressed groups to eliminate the barriers between themselves and people of minority status. Society functions at a higher level when white people learn to be comfortable with people of color, when straights stop discriminating against gays, when Christians develop tolerance for Jews and Muslims (who are minorities in the U.S. but not elsewhere in the world), when people who can walk create access for people who use wheelchairs, and so on. As an organizer, if you experience diversity among your prospective clients but, somehow, those who become actual clients are all just like you, you might be making discriminatory choices.

In the helping professions, respect for diversity is a paramount component of client dignity and welfare. Discrimination, bias, and prejudicial thinking are considered repugnant. Helping professionals are of course recognized as human, complete with the influence of familial and societal biases, but they are expected to search for and root out their biases before those ideas can infect and hinder their client work. It violates the definition of a helping professional to think less of or offer less service to a client because the person is the "wrong" gender, ethnicity, religion, class, sexual orientation, etc.

However, you're not a licensed helping professional (e.g. a social worker, therapist, or counselor, unless you are that in addition to an organizer), and so it could be argued that you don't have to think as they are expected to think. It would be defensible to say that you don't have to eradicate every bit of biased thinking you may have; all you really have to do is prevent it from harming a client. For that you have two options: Take the client and make darned sure you can hide your bias, or make a compassionate referral to another organizer. Ignoring voicemails from prospective clients who sound like they're the "wrong" type is not okay.

If you do aspire to be bias-free, know that doing so is one of the surest ways to support the ethical tenet of client dignity and welfare.

2. Boundaries of Competence

Your boundaries of competence are the limits of what you are able to do. Of course, this leads to several questions, including "How well do I have to do it?" That's why it's plural—you have varying levels of competence and therefore several key boundaries.

Imagine a set of concentric circles. The center area (the "bull's-eye") contains everything at which you are highly skilled. The ring around that center contains everything at which you are able to do a decent job. The next ring contains everything that you do poorly for whatever reason (lack of innate ability, lack of training or practice, loss of skill, etc.).

The last, outside ring contains everything you've seen or heard about but never tried, whether common (like a sport) or implausible (like flying a space shuttle). You can rank everything you do, both professionally and personally, according to these levels: highly competent, competent, incompetent, and unknown.

Those things that you do as a professional organizer are what are relevant to this ethical tenet. For every job and every task with each client, your competence varies. Now, a simple, black-and-white rule about this could be, "Do only those things at which you are highly competent."

Sounds good, but it's impossible. In professional organizing, as in most things, you have to work your way up from incompetence, and at least some of that development has to be with real clients. The key to doing this ethically is managing the amount of risk your "practice" poses for the client.

In many situations, the chance that you will cause harm to the client due to inexperience is quite low and is mitigated, or offset, by other factors. For example, suppose you are a brand-new organizer and you offer to organize the storage room at your community center, for free, to get experience. Say it takes you 15 hours to do it—five times as long as it will take you to do an equivalent job a year from now. If you had charged by the hour for that time, it could be argued that there was harm to the community center because it paid for 15 hours with an incompetent organizer instead of 3 hours with a competent one. But since you charged nothing, and assuming there were no other potential risks to the client, there was no harm.

Supervision

In the mental health professions, they have a system for mitigating risk as new practitioners develop competence. It's called supervision. This is not supervision in the employment sense, where you have a boss or manager to answer to. Rather, this form of supervision is more like very structured mentoring. In mental health, people working at hospitals, large practices, and treatment facilities have a clinical supervisor assigned to them. In private practice (which is most like what we do as organizers), clinicians hire their own supervisor.

"What? The worker pays the supervisor? Isn't that backwards?" That was my first reaction when I heard about this system. Now, though, I see the sense in it.

Suppose you are a new organizer with very little experience. You've completed some jobs with low client risk that helped you to build your competence, but now you've been asked to help a client who is deaf. You have no personal or past work experience with hearing-impaired people. You've been told that this client has some ability to read lips and can speak, but new people usually find it difficult to understand him. There is no other organizer in the area who has experience specifically with deaf clients, so there is no obvious referral to be made.

At this point, you might think you have two choices: decline, or wing it. Actually, you have a third choice, and it is the best one: Take the client and obtain some supervision.

Supervision is the solution to that outer ring of the competence circle—the one containing all the things you've never tried. In our example, if you begin by consulting with an experienced organizer and/or with someone in a relevant outside field such as speech therapy, and you touch base with that person periodically as you work with the client, you are demonstrating a conscientious approach to mitigating risk while developing competence in a new area.

Obviously, there are limits to the amount of risk that supervision can mitigate. It would be unwise to tell a client you can perform his appendectomy because you talked to a surgeon about it. Your ethical obligation when pushing your boundaries of competence is to determine whether supervision will offset the risk enough to make it ethical for you to proceed.

Chronic Disorganization

In professional organizing, chronic disorganization is a specialization that carries significant risk to the client if done without well-established competence. This is one area where winging it is definitely unethical—a boundary violation, not just a boundary crossing. The Institute for Challenging Disorganization (ICD) has developed a tool to help organizers assess their boundaries of competence with chronically disorganized clients. The ICD Clutter-Hoarding Scale quantifies the amount and type of clutter in a home, ranking it from Level I to Level V. The ICD gives recommendations for the amount of experience and training an organizer should have to work with each of the five levels, and it offers extensive education on the many facets of chronic disorganization to help organizers develop competence in working with these challenging clients.

3. Confidentiality

This is an ethical tenet that many organizers overlook. Your clients have the right to complete privacy in their dealings with you—everything from their name to the contents of their nightstand. I've seen many organizers react with genuine surprise at the idea that they shouldn't talk about their clients by name and that they should think carefully about lettering on their vehicles and before-and-after photos on their websites.

If you consider the level of confidentiality to which you are legally entitled at a doctor's or therapist's office, you can begin to see what is also ideal in our industry. Clients should be able to have no one know they're working with you if that is their preference, and you should assume it is their preference unless they tell you otherwise. This dovetails with our fifth ethical tenet, Informed Consent.

Your obligation to provide confidentiality extends to your own data, including the electronic files and paper documents on your desk, in your office drawers, on devices such as your computer, cellphone, or tablet, or as paper or portable electronic files carried in your car or bag. There have been many hair-raising cases in the news about customer financial data that was lost or stolen by the companies to whom it was entrusted; many of those companies ended up criminally liable for their failure to protect the data. If you store clients' credit card or bank account information, you have the legal responsibility to protect it. By the same token, if you store private information about them, including personal details such as diagnoses, relationship status, work troubles, or anything else that could be considered sensitive, embarrassing, or simply nobody else's business, you have at least an ethical and possibly also a legal obligation not to deliberately reveal that information and to take reasonable measures to keep it secure from unintentional disclosure.

4. Dual Relationships

If you fill two distinct roles with a client, you have a dual relationship with that person. Dual relationships are not automatically verboten, but they are an ethical boundary crossing because, by their nature, they create the possibility of a conflict of interest. Some common examples of dual relationships in professional organizing include:

• Doing one-on-one consultation and also representing a product;

• Working with two clients who have a relationship with each other;

- Working with a client who has influence over you, such as your college professor;

- Working with a client over whom you have power, e.g. if you started your organizing business by soliciting clients from among your staff at your previous job;

- Organizing someone to whom you are also a client, such as your computer maintenance consultant or web designer;

- Organizing your own family member;

- Serving as a client's organizer and also their housekeeper or babysitter;

- Socializing as friends with a client.

Perhaps the riskiest of all dual relationships is dating a client. If either the professional or the personal part of the relationship goes bad, it's almost certain to take the other half with it. In the licensed helping professions, the ethical priority is always the client's wellbeing, which makes the professional relationship paramount—so much so, in fact, that intimate relationships with clients are among the worst possible ethical violations for mental health care providers.

Again, here is an example of a way in which the profundity of professional organizing and mental health care can be very different or remarkably the same, depending on the nature of the organizing work. If you meet an eligible bachelorette when you present a one-time seminar at her company and three weeks later she asks you to lunch, that's a very different scenario than if you spend six months helping a depressed, chronically disorganized woman clear out a roomful of clutter so she can sleep in her bed, and then you celebrate by jumping in with her.

Let me reiterate: Not all dual relationships in professional organizing are bad, ill-advised, or unethical. Remember, every ethical question depends on context. There are many organizers among us who profit from reselling a product and also work one-on-one with clients, all while avoiding conflicts of interest with grace and ease. Rather than automatically rejecting such a business model, or in fact most any dual relationship, I encourage you to consider all of your options, including any potential ethical complications that you would need to prepare for and avoid in order to make the dual relationship safe. In some cases, this will include having to work extra-hard to demonstrate your objectivity and commitment to the client's needs and priorities.

Still, if there is any possibility, even the most remote, that having a second type of relationship with a client could cause the client harm, pain, discomfort, distraction, anxiety, or any other negative, it would be unethical to do it. Consider the implications for yourself too: If you might be the one who is harmed, you should avoid it for your own good but also because any negatives for you would likely damage the client relationship, resulting once again in possible harm to the client.

5. Informed Consent

This concept means, in broad terms, that we must always give the client all of the information that is relevant to their decision on whether to work with us. Clients must be fully informed of everything they are consenting to. This includes basic things like your fees and cancellation policy, and it also includes less obvious topics like your background, amount of training and experience, and philosophies about your work, as well as operational issues like how you will contact them, what you will say if their friends or family ask how they're progressing, and how you will use any feedback they give you. In short, clients have the right to know, to the fullest extent that it can be predicted, exactly what they're getting into when they choose to work with you.

This ethical tenet also provides an excellent illustration of the inherent power imbalance that exists between the client and the professional organizer (or any consultant). The concept of informed consent requires a bit more than the literal informing of the client and their consenting to that information: It also requires framing the exchange in such a way that the client actually has the power to provide consent freely.

It is important to realize that we are indeed in a position of power over our clients. Clients look to us as experts, and many tend to imbue us with more authority and credibility than we have actually earned. In a phenomenon called the halo effect, their good impression of our organizing skills leads them to assume that we have expertise in other areas and provokes an overall willingness to comply with our suggestions and requests. What all of this means is that when you ask clients to do something for you, such as write a testimonial or allow you to take photos, many will do it even if they're uncomfortable because they've put their trust in you and your expertise. Manipulating or capitalizing on that trust for your own benefit, even if it's not clearly detrimental to them, is unethical.

The ethically conservative way to manage this power imbalance is to decide that there are some things you will never ask of clients because you can't be certain they would feel totally free to respond honestly. For example, a personal policy of mine is that I will never ask a client to join me for an interview with a reporter (something almost every reporter requests). In the mental health professions, this choice would be well-supported by existing codes of ethics; in fact, to make such a request of a client would be a significant boundary crossing, if not an outright boundary violation. In professional organizing, with our codes of ethics as they are, it remains up to each of us to make such decisions.

6. Intellectual Property

This is an area that, in my impression, seems not to be one of frequent violation in mental health, but unfortunately it has become quite a problem in the organizing field. Unlike most of the other issues covered in this book, this one also has legal implications—and it is addressed precisely in the NAPO, BCPO, and ICD codes of ethics.

A Very Brief Primer

A person's intellectual property is anything that they have invented, written, designed, recorded, or otherwise created. This book is my intellectual property, and as such I hold the copyright to it.

However, there are things in this book that don't actually belong to me. This font, for example, probably belongs to Microsoft. I get to use it without attribution, or credit, because I purchased a license to the software that contains it and that license allows such usage. The same is true of the template in which this book was composed.

I did not take the photograph on the cover, so it is not my intellectual property, even though it appears with my intellectual property. (I purchased the right to use it and I credited the photographer in the frontmatter.) Similarly, my headshot on the back cover is not my intellectual property because I did not take it, but it is my legal property. The agreement I made with the photographer, which is standard for commercial portraits, transferred her rights completely to me, so I don't even have to credit her. Other examples of things within this book that are not my intellectual property include everything I have quoted (utilizing the legal exception to copyright restriction known as the "Fair Use Doctrine") or referenced (and cited, to respect the rights of the person to whom it does belong).

Now for the trickiest part: Even though the cover photo, the quotes, the font, etc., do not actually belong to me, no one else can use them in the exact same way that I have, because that unique combination of them DOES now belong to me: It is my intellectual property. If you wrote a book and gave it a title similar to mine, bought the same photo for your cover, or created a similar design and you crossed the ill-defined line between "different enough" and "too much alike," or if you used any of my words without attribution or beyond fair use, I would be giving you a call (see Chapter 5). Likewise if you leaned heavily on this book in a class of your own without crediting me, or if you created a class based entirely on this book, even if you did credit me. I'm using myself as a hypothetical example here, but my sympathies are with those colleagues who have been the victims of these actual violations.

I know these rules because I completed a degree in journalism and I spent ten years working for a publishing firm before starting my organizing business. Regrettably, most of my fellow organizers do not have this knowledge, so we are pretty much all at risk of both committing and being the victim of all forms of intellectual property theft, including plagiarism, copyright infringement, and trademark infringement. Equally unfortunate are the opportunities we miss by being too careful: The Fair Use Doctrine allows us to quote, within certain parameters (albeit very imprecise ones), portions of each other's works in the interest of disseminating knowledge. I have had many well-meaning, conservative colleagues contact me to ask permission to name a book of mine in their own work—something for which permission is not needed—and I despair of how many others have just not used it because they thought it was forbidden. Intellectual property is a topic about which we have an urgent need for intra-industry education.

The Ethical Component

Even though it might be understandable for an organizer to be uninformed about intellectual property rights, it is nonetheless unethical to violate them. Surely you know what plagiarism is—we've been taught since elementary school not to "copy off each other." You should also realize that buying one copy of someone's publication, audio recording, or video recording and making copies of it for distribution beyond fair use is both illegal and unethical. If you distribute those copies for a fee, you're committing a serious federal offense.

If you are unclear on the restrictions of intellectual property, copyright, and trademarks, or on the leeway afforded by Fair Use, I encourage you to look them up and learn more.

In the interim, you will cover a lot of ethical ground if you remember simply to give credit where credit is due. If you read a theory or technique in a book or hear it in a class, you are allowed, welcome even, to reference it with attribution, i.e. with credit to the person who created it, whenever you give a speech, add content to your website, develop a class, write a book of your own, or otherwise create intellectual property.

However, when you're working with a client and utilizing that theory or technique, you are not duty-bound to tell the client where it came from. It is often useful to share the origins of theories with clients for their further study, but it would be tedious to the point of counterproductivity and probably impossible to cite every piece of your knowledge back to its origins. Do remember, though, that whether you give the history or not, you cannot claim that you created something if you didn't.

It is common to forget where you learned something or even to think you came up with it on your own. There was a concept I included in an early version of my NAPO class "OD1-101: Fundamental Organizing & Productivity Principles" that I had either forgotten or never known came from Stephen Covey, author of *The Seven Habits of Highly Effective People* (1989). When someone said they thought it was his, I did some digging and finally, sure enough, found it in one of his books and added the attribution to my teaching notes and the course workbook. Such unintended errors are more human lapse than ethical violation, but they're still best avoided. If someone points out that you've made such an error, my suggestion would be to correct it immediately and humbly and, going forward, pay closer attention to the origins of what you learn so can credit them accurately when you create intellectual property of your own.

7. Manner of Compensation

Here is a category with a surprising amount of ethical complication. You might think that if you are charging a fair price, that is all you need to do to be ethical, but there is actually much more to it. The relatively straightforward matter of your fee is just the tip of the iceberg.

Speaking of your fee, we need to avoid speaking of it. Although the mental health codes of ethics are generally much more comprehensive and stricter than those of professional organizing, this point presents one notable way in which organizing is far more conservative. NAPO regularly reminds members not to give the dollar amount of their fees in conversation with one another, because to do so could be construed as the illegal practice of price-fixing, or agreeing on a minimum price that everyone should charge. I have asked several mental health practitioners about this and they've told me that they are not aware of such a concern in their field. I haven't yet figured out what accounts for this difference, so I remain conservative and follow NAPO's advice, both as an organizer and as a counselor.

With that agreed, let's consider some of the ethical complications around the ways in which you could be compensated or indirectly rewarded for your organizing work. Ironically, the gag order on open discussion of rates casts a shadow over some problems and allows them to grow like tenacious fungi: With no peer-to-peer accountability, it is possible for an organizer to set their rates unjustly, doing things like practicing price-gouging when the opportunity arises or quoting an astronomical rate for clients against whom they're biased.

Referral fees, another standard practice in our industry, can become an ethical problem if a client goes unserved because no organizer in their area was willing to pay a fee to the person or agency attempting to refer them. Who is unethical in such a case? The organizer who refuses the referral because it comes with a fee, or the person who will only forward the referral if the fee is paid?

Bartering, another compensation option, also carries some ethical risks. One is that it creates a dual relationship, as discussed above. Other possibilities include potential disagreements over the number of hours or amount of credit one party owes the other; it stands to reason that the organizer will be better at keeping track of such things, which creates an additional imbalance of power. Ending the relationship also becomes complicated: How can a client feel free to "fire" you if one of you owes the other barter credits?

Gifts also create ethical issues in this category. Whether you give them to clients or they give them to you, there is an impact on your professional relationship. Remember that you have a degree of inherent power over your clients. If you give a client a gift, might they feel obligated to give you one in return? If a client gives you a gift and you have never expressed a policy against it, could you decline now and be sure the client is not offended or hurt? Or if a client gives you a gift and you're delighted to take it, might the client be inclined to give you more and more?

By the way, if you're wondering whether used belongings the client gives to you are considered gifts, the answer is yes.

8. Responsibility to the Profession

After we have satisfied our multitudinous ethical responsibilities to our clients, we have still more in the form of responsibilities to our profession. These constitute our duty to behave ethically toward our peers, employees or subcontractors, supervisees and consultees, and associates in other professions.

This is the section that closes the loophole of individual harm. It is possible to make the argument that some so-called unethical behaviors are "victimless" because they do not harm a client, and so they should not be considered unethical at all. However, someone long ago discovered the flaw in this logic and refuted it with the observation that even if a bad apple does not spoil the entire barrel, it still gives apples a bad name.

Cherishing your clients does not make you ethical if you also abuse your colleagues. If you only have so much care to go around, I myself would rather you reserve it for your clients and treat me poorly since they would suffer more under your power, but I can't issue that permission on behalf of all your colleagues, and it still wouldn't make it okay anyway.

We represent our profession more directly than many others. Professional organizing is a unique industry, one with a lot of public interest and a rather high profile. It is also a young, unproven industry with a comparatively low number of practitioners. For many people, whether client or other professional, you are the first and last organizer they will ever meet, so you embody their single direct impression of the organizing industry. That gives us each a grave ethical responsibility to personify honor on behalf of one another individually and on behalf of our industry as a collective self.

CHAPTER 3: PITFALL SCENARIOS

Now for some sticky situations. As you read these scenarios, try to identify any ethical problems that are demonstrated or alluded to in them, and also apply some foresight: What ethical problems could be encountered in the future if the situation continues on its current path? Which of the key ethical tenets and moral principles are involved in each?

I've grouped these potential pitfalls according to when you're likely to encounter them, but there is a great deal of overlap among them: Residential dilemmas could occur in business settings, media encounters could happen when you're off-duty, and so on.

As you read the vignettes, try to imagine how you could end up in a similar situation. Many of them stop at a crossroads, implying the question, "What will you do?" Don't think it can't happen to you—everyone encounters ethical problems, and sometimes they sneak up when we least expect it! In fact, without the story to stop you, you might have just flown right through these crossroads without realizing their significance, whether you're a brand-new organizer or a twenty-year veteran. Remember, the hardest part of ethical thought is recognizing when you have an ethical problem. It's tough to know what you don't know, and there isn't much you can do about it if you're blind to it. Use these scenarios to sharpen your ethical focus.

For an advanced challenge, try to think of a way to make each story turn out okay. Can you divert an ethical train wreck and actually transform the situation into a win for everyone?

Don't bother looking for an answer key in the back of the book—there isn't one. Remember, the way you would address each situation depends on its context and your unique application of ethical theory. There is always more than one right answer, so giving you an answer key would defeat our purpose here. (And, yes, I admit I enjoyed creating a bunch of fine messes for YOU to clean up!)

When Working with Clients

Barb the Builder

Barb is a columns-and-rows kind of gal, so she adores modular closets. She outfitted all of her own closets at home with the Easy Track do-it-yourself system, and she got so confident that now she wants to offer this service to her clients. When people ask how she learned to do it, she proudly declares that she is completely self-taught—she had never picked up a tool before, and now she even has her own table saw.

It's One of Our Perks

Sheri is talking to another woman who came to this month's NAPO chapter meeting. "It's one of the perks of this business," she says. "Usually what they get rid of is junk, but sometimes it's really great stuff that they just don't want any more. Sometimes they just want an excuse to buy something new! I've gotten clothes, a printer . . . even a set of china that I'm sure is worth a lot of money. That particular client is really rich, so she didn't care."

A Token of Appreciation

A few organizers at a regional conference are talking about gifts. "I always send my clients a three-hour gift certificate for Christmas," says one. "Me too," says another, "plus a Starbuck's card." Joining the conversation, you ask, "What do you do for Jewish clients?" The first organizer gives you a blank look and then says, "Uh, I don't have any." "I just do Christmas for everyone," says the second. "It's not just a religious holiday."

Surprise, It's Me!

"What a nice son," you think as you hang up. He just hired you to work with his mother for ten hours as a birthday gift. He wants to surprise her, so he's going to take her to brunch that day and leave the door unlocked so you can get started on the living room. When they get back, she'll be able to step through the door and see a big change.

Why Is She Crying?

So far your clients have been pretty normal, but this new one. . . . What a downer. She argues about every little piece of junk and today she actually started crying. Sheesh! You're thinking about being "too busy" to give her another appointment.

Is That What I Think It Is?

"Shoot, why didn't I just wait?" The client had to take a bathroom break and she left you sitting on the bedroom floor, sorting books from under the bed. You finished that and, since you can't stand doing nothing, you started pulling more books out of the nightstand. Now you're holding a spiral notebook with a loose wire on one end, which snagged a hole in a quart-size zipper bag of please-be-oregano which then spilled into your lap.

Let's Talk about Your Childhood

You've been working with Agnes for about a year now, and her progress has been really slow, but she has made some. She's chronically disorganized, and together you've gotten her home from a Level IV down to a Level III on the Clutter-Hoarding Scale—no small feat. You've been endlessly encouraging and she trusts you, but she still just can't stop belittling herself for her housekeeping, paper management, bargain-hunting, cooking, and every other household management skill. She often mentions how perfect her mother was, and it's obvious that is the root of all of this. You're thinking maybe you should just talk to her about it and try to help her get past it.

An Authorized Reseller

Passive income is a great thing; you only get a few cents or dollars from each click-through agreement for links on your website, but together they add up to nothing to sneeze at. Along the same lines, you've agreed to represent some products for a percentage of sales. It's legitimate business, so why did your client today seem so suspicious? He needs a new filing system and the File-a-Rino would be great for him. When you told him all about it, though, he seemed unconvinced. You listed all the advantages, which make the price well worth it, and he replied, "Uh huh. And how much do you get from that?

I Think He Means It

Did you hear that right? The prospective client just said he'd like to burn his house down, and he didn't laugh. Other clients have made similar remarks in jest or despair, but this sounded different. He said he knows "all this crap" is a fire hazard, and he smokes in bed, he says, hoping he'll fall asleep and "finally escape."

Spare the Rod

Your client seems especially grim today. You noticed that her husband's car was out front; he's not usually home at this time. You ask her if everything is ok and she nods. He stomps through the kitchen as you're pulling pans out of a cabinet; she freezes. Down the hall you hear a door slam. She starts talking all of a sudden, about how much she loves this brand of cookware. More noises down the hall, yelling and some thuds, then the music gets louder. She fires one question after another and pulls your attention into the work. As you're leaving, you glance down the hall and see their eight-year-old son limping across to the bathroom.

Chapter 3

They're Just Too Lazy

Y'know, to see it on TV, you would really think disorganized people want to straighten themselves up and are grateful for professional help. But your clients just don't seem to care that much. Why is it they almost never do their homework? You ask and they just shuffle their feet and make excuses. It's really not that difficult—you just have to want it badly enough. So why do they bother calling you if they aren't willing to do the work?

Oscar and Felix

Your new client is an older woman who lives with a female friend. Neither one has kids. (You're starting to think they're a lesbian couple, but, does that happen with senior citizens?) The client is a saver, and it drives her roommate nuts; in fact, the roommate keeps pulling you aside and saying things like, "You're going to make her throw all this junk out, right?" They're both acting exasperated but they're not talking about it, at least not while you're there.

Blood Out of Stones

You've been hired to do a full day of consulting for a local design firm: a morning time-management workshop, lunchtime q & a, and afternoon one-on-one sessions with the "problem" employees. By midday, you've figured out that the company's challenges do not match the picture painted for you by the HR manager: These employees aren't disorganized; they're being worked to death. Now you're expected to coach three "underperformers" in how to reach their (humanly impossible) production assignments through better organization.

Over Your Head

She said she had a lot of stuff, but, whoa. Now that you've seen it, your confidence is shaken. And cats too—she said she has three cats, but you know you saw more than that. Could it be that she actually doesn't realize how many there are? She definitely needs more help than you can give. But, gosh, it was so hard to get her even this far—several phone calls, some an hour long, and a couple of rescheduled appointments before she was finally comfortable with letting you come over. She finally seems to trust you. How is she going to feel if you hand her off to someone else?

A Little Too "Springer"

This has gotten just too crazy. At first you were working with the wife only, and the husband made occasional cracks about her being a slob, but otherwise he pretty much stayed out of it. Then he wanted your help in the garage, and the wife came in and mocked him: "What's wrong, Mr. Perfect, I thought you said professional organizers are for slackers." Now it seems they're competing for your approval, making some really nasty remarks about each other, and neither one likes it when you say they're both doing great. You won't be surprised if they start throwing chairs like they're on *Jerry Springer*.

Let's Just See How It Goes

You are not one of those left-brain/linear professional organizers. Some structure is a good thing, but too much is just, well, too much. This is why you prefer to let your client sessions unfold naturally—let the client's mood and needs that day dictate your work. Sometimes a client will spend some time going in circles, and very often they forget what their original intentions were with hiring you, but that's okay because the value is in experiencing the process, not so much in some specific end result.

The Only Help He Can Afford

Mel is such a sweet old guy. It's a shame his wife died since his kids live out of state and he's all alone now. He manages to pay for your help with the mail and bills once a month, but he certainly has to be careful now that he's down to just his social security. Last week he got a notice in the mail of some issue with his taxes—something about her death and the meager life insurance payout he got. He sure can't afford an accountant, so you're going to look into it for him.

WHAT ELSE CAN YOU ADD FROM YOUR OWN CLIENT CASES?

When Managing Your Business

They All Look So Good

"Hmm. This is tough—like choosing just a few electives back in school. They all sound so interesting." You're filling out your NAPO membership application and trying to limit yourself to the ten specialty categories included at no extra charge. You want to choose wisely, since this list will be seen by prospective clients coming to the NAPO website for a referral. What types of clients do you want to attract? You know it would be smart to try for repeat business, not just one-time projects. "Chronically disorganized. That sounds stable. And ADHD. Those poor folks will need a lot of help. Yes, definitely those two. Now what else? . . ."

Say It Loud, I'm a PO and Proud

"Uh . . . would you mind moving your car?" You parked in the driveway and the new client is eyeing your Suburban like it's contagious. "Sure, no problem," you reply, wondering what's the problem. "On the street?" "Yes, please, on the other side." "That's fine," you think as you parallel park it, "my new lettering will be more noticeable out here anyway."

Making Faces

What did businesses ever do without the Internet? Just being able to use these animated characters is a great innovation. They're really eye-catching the way they gasp and cry next to your "Before" pictures. Your website is so much more impactful than those brochures you used to have.

The Lost Laptop

"This can't be happening." The police met you at Starbuck's. "I got here about an hour ago and I was working at this table, and there was this nice lady sitting over here. I asked her to watch my laptop while I ran to the restroom, and when I came back, the computer was gone and so was she." They're asking you to describe her. What did she look like? "Nice! She looked exactly like nice! Arrgh!" You were working on client files—think, are the company names in there? The password! You have one, but it engages with the screen saver and that takes five minutes. You weren't even in the bathroom five minutes. This is NOT happening. . . .

Anywhere but There

You're trying to figure out how to describe your client coverage area. You live in Ypsilanti, Michigan, and you don't want to say you cover the entire county because the northwest corner is too far. You also don't want to limit yourself to just your city—that would be too narrow. You could say you cover a range of 25 miles, but then you might get calls from Detroit, and that's what you're trying to avoid.

It's in the Bag

You took the CPO® exam last week and you know you aced it—you had studied well, and every question on there was familiar. You won't get the actual results for a while yet, but it's time to renew your Chamber of Commerce directory ad, and if you don't add your new credential now, you'll have to wait another entire year.

You Make My Files, I'll Make Yours

Your new BNI membership is already paying off. This week the web designer approached you and said he really needs help with his paper files, and he noticed that your business card doesn't list a website. Would you by chance be needing one? Perfect—as a matter of fact, you do need a website. It seems unnecessary to trade money when you could just trade services, but you've never bartered before. You can't say why, but you're a little uneasy about it.

The Best Organizer on the Planet

OK, maybe not that, but your business consultant wants you to be bold, drop the false modesty, and give yourself some sort of superlative. What will you be? The premier professional organizer in the county? The best in the state? The most respected in the region? The top choice of metro businesses? The best trained? The most qualified?

And How Are the Curtises This Week?

Your husband does the Quicken data entry for your personal accounts, so when you started your business it was natural for him to do your bookkeeping. Each week as he enters your clients' payments, he inquires about their progress. He's really pulling for Reggie and Lu Curtis, but he's not too fond of Toby Gordon.

A Discriminatory Rule

You thought certification would be a great step forward for the industry, adding a large measure of credibility and validation which professional organizing both needs and deserves. However, you never thought that you, a ten-year veteran, would be deemed ineligible. They require you to have had 1500 client hours in the last five years; you did that in your first three years, and many hundreds more since then, and your business has grown to include not just client work but also speaking, writing, and peer coaching. To your mind, that makes you even more credible, not less, but it limits your direct client contact time, and that's their big yardstick. You could just take the test and hope they don't audit your records to prove those hours. . . .

Chicken and Egg

You're browsing other organizers' websites, looking for some fresh ideas for yours, when you read a passage that sounds very familiar. You realize it sounds like something you wrote for . . . what was it? The chapter newsletter? Something in the local paper? You do a text search on your computer and find it—sure enough, it's word for word. But what if this other organizer says you stole it from HER?

They Love Me, They Really Do

The marketing guru who spoke at your business women's luncheon said you need to promote yourself with testimonials from satisfied clients, so you've been writing it down each time a client says thanks or tells you how happy they are. You've got their quotes, names, and cities all ready to add to your website. You've even figured out how to make them scroll across the top of each page. This is going to be great for business!

Excuse Me, I Believe That's Mine

You self-published a book about organizing for scrapbook enthusiasts like yourself, and it's developed quite a nice little fanbase online. What an unpleasant surprise it was when, during a weekend "crop" event at a local hotel, you went to a workshop in which the speaker based her presentation on . . . your book!

A Sliding Scale

You don't understand the idea of setting one rate for every client. Wouldn't it be fairer to charge them based on what they can afford? Other businesses have sliding-scale fee structures. If a person can't afford your lowest rate, that's one thing, but for some of them even your highest rate is a pittance. Why shouldn't they pay more?

WHAT ELSE COULD TRIP UP YOUR OPERATIONS? DRAFT
MORE BUSINESS MANAGEMENT SCENARIOS

When Interacting with Peers

Safety First?

"Ugh, please don't ever call back," you think as you hang up. The caller said his company is relocating to Anaheim, California, and he wants an organizer to help him prepare to sell his condo and move. However, he also said he really wishes he had a wife to take with him, asked if you're married, and complimented your website photo. You pretended to check your calendar and told him you're booked for the next month. He asked if you're at least free for dinner, and when you told him no, he muttered a few expletives and hung up. A week later, you're at a chapter meeting and a colleague asks if you know anything about Anaheim, California.

Ooh, Good Dirt!

It's Tuesday at noon, so it must be time for the weekly organizers luncheon at Panera. You're in line to order and the group spots you. Benito hollers over: "Leslie, you are so not gonna believe this— wait'll you hear what those crazy Averys did this week!" Hurray, good dirt! These lunches are always such fun!

What's in a Name?

You're the chapter's membership director, so the new member applications come to you. You're entering one into the database when you notice the person has chosen a company name that's the same as someone who's already a member—someone you really don't like.

Cash Cows

You and Larry have this running joke. You're fortunate to each have one longstanding client with unlimited funds and no real organizational problems who basically pays you for your friendship, so whenever you see Larry, you greet him with "How's your cash cow?" and he always responds, "UDDERly fine, and yours?" A little organizers' inside humor.

The Virtual Library

The book you wanted came in print and PDF formats, and you ordered the PDF to save a tree (or at least a branch). Within 24 hours, the file arrived via email. You mentioned it to a board member of your chapter and she said, "I've heard of that one. Could you forward it to me?" Now you're wondering, is that the same as lending her a print copy, or should she buy her own?

The Burden of Power

You've been asked to join your chapter's Nominations Committee. One of your best business friends really wants to be president and expects that you will vouch for her, but you secretly think she's a poor choice for the job.

Cleaning Up after Delilah

Another half-baked, so-called system. She might as well spray-paint "DeeDee Wuz Here" on her clients' walls: Every other organizer in the county has seen the destruction she wreaks and can tell it was her even before the client says, "Did you, um, take the same training as Delilah Jingleheimer-Schmidt?" Now you have to not only help the client rebuild her file system in a way that actually will make a lick of sense, but you also have to rehabilitate the reputation of the industry with this client and encourage her to go back to all the friends and family she complained to about DeeDee, and tell them that the next organizer actually did have a clue.

What's My Line?

"Hey, I like that," you think as a colleague wraps up her round-robin introduction with a memorable catchphrase. "I think I'll use that too." Next month, you end your intro with it, but instead of smiling, your colleagues are looking puzzled. Did you mis-pronounce it? Oh well, you'll get more polished over time.

Thanks for Your Support

You told the new associate member that you really like his product. The chapter posted his logo to the homepage of the website, and he's asking individual members to do the same. At the last meeting, he publicly thanked each person who had given him a link; you avoided eye contact when he looked your way. You really do like it, but you've just never gotten comfortable with endorsing products.

She's Giving It Away

Great, there's another cheap newbie in town. You called the prospective client who emailed you through the NAPO automated referral system, and he said he'd found someone already but, "by the way," he asked, "what do you charge?" When you told him your rate, he said, "Oh, OK, Shaundra charges much less. OK, well, thanks for calling!"

BRAINSTORM SOME MORE POSSIBILITIES WITH YOUR PEERS

When Dealing with the Media

Who Wouldn't Want Free Help?

A TV reporter you've worked with a couple times calls with an idea: Would you like to do an "Extreme Makeover"-type of show? You'd get to choose the client of yours who is most in need and the station would pay you to do the entire job and provide supplies, filming the whole thing to air as a one-hour special. You have a client in mind who is very shy, but to get all of this for free, you think she might go for it. And what great exposure for your business and the industry!

Give Us Dirty Laundry

The reporter wants to interview you, but she needs you to think of an idea for illustrating the story. She asks if you have any "hoarder clients—even if we could get just a picture of a mess in the yard." She promises the house will be out of focus in the background. You understand their dilemma—a picture really is worth a thousand words.

Sunday Morning Confession

You're scheduled to appear on the local Sunday morning news. Spring is approaching and the reporter wants to talk about clearing out the clutter that builds up over the winter. "OK, confession time," he says, "my car is a pit right now. Who wants to stand out in the cold long enough to clean it out? Of course, that doesn't explain my basement, but I bet it's nowhere near the worst you've ever seen!" He looks to you for your reaction.

I've Got a Blog and I Know How to Use It

Reporters usually do a good job of quoting you, but this latest one really biffed it. For the first time ever, you actually called the editor and asked for a retraction, but he told you they only do that in the event of factual errors, not arguments of interpretation or "quotes you regret in hindsight." Grr! Of course, journalism today is not the exclusive domain of the publishing companies. Perhaps this calls for a well-worded blog post.

A Star Is Born

Your daughter, who is working on a bachelor's in journalism, just started her internship with the local cable company. Her job is to develop new ideas for public-access shows, and she suggested you for a show about organizing. Who knew such an opportunity was right there in your town? They even have a studio and editing equipment available for their public-access personalities. Today you're taping "reaction shots" — surprised, disgusted, frightened, proud, delighted, confused—that they'll keep on file to splice into your upcoming episodes recorded "on location" with real clients.

Basking in Reflected Expertise

Your first interview went very well, thank you very much! You even got the chance to mention the "Up, Down, & Over" technique. Thank goodness you reread that book *Organizing Sets My Heart on Fire* last week! You couldn't think of the author's name in the moment, but you figure that's one of those "general organizing knowledge" ideas anyway.

HOW ELSE COULD PUBLICITY BE A PITFALL?

When Off-Duty

"TP" Thinking*

Your mother's at it again. "Dear, how in the world do you tolerate Those People and their messes? It can't be healthy for you to be around all that dust and mold all the time. George, tell her." Your dad knows better than to argue. "Hon, listen to your mother. Why can't they throw away their own trash? Or just call a maid service? I thought you said you don't do cleaning." You've been through this so many times, and they just don't get it. Mercifully, your brother changes the subject. Later, though, driving home and alone with your thoughts, you admit it's true: It is pretty disgusting how These People live.

*Thanks to Jennifer McDaniel-Wolfe for coining this phrase with me.

Train the Trainer?

You've been going to physical therapy for three months now (you knew you shouldn't have lifted that client's desk), and today one of the assistants said to your therapist, "Don't forget to ask him." "Oh, right," the therapist says, "we were hoping you could take a look at the boss's office. He could really use your expertise. Hey, you call that a push-up?" Ten reps later, you're squeezed around the boss's desk with the therapist, the assistant, and the office manager, who is pointing at paper piles and making little squeals of disgust, when the boss appears in the doorway.

Good Prospects

They said you needed to get out and meet more people, and this business has turned out to be a great way to do it! Some of your clients have such charming brothers, friends, and coworkers, and they've been keeping your weekends very busy. The client you started with today mentioned her son and you noticed his picture on the mantel—very handsome! You're hoping to add him to your dance card.

Shut Up Already

It's getting to the point that you don't want to tell people what you do. You are so sick and tired of everyone assuming you're anal-retentive, obsessive-compulsive, a control freak with a picture-perfect home and seven picture-perfect kids who line up to sing "Edelweiss" at bedtime every night. Now here you are at the PTA meeting and yet another other mother has said, "A professional organizer? Oh, yikes, you're never coming to my house!"

On Second Thought

You're making your usual Saturday afternoon trip to Goodwill; seems like you're wearing a path from your house to their loading dock. You're glad to be able to help your clients offload so much stuff they don't need, but schlepping it to the site is getting kind of old. As you wait for Louie (yep, you two are on first-name terms) to come to your trunk with his clipboard, you open the lid of a box to remind yourself what's inside. "Hey!" you mentally exclaim, "I didn't realize she finally decided to toss that. No wonder she practically threw the box at me and said, 'Donate it before I change my mind.' She is definitely a paper-planner person. Look at that, the charger's here and everything. Mine is getting pretty old. I wonder if this one has more memory. . . ."

The Business That Refused to Die

You tried professional organizing, but it just wasn't for you, so you closed up shop over a year ago. You got yourself off the NAPO website, but somehow people are still finding your number and email, and some past clients have called you back too. At first you gave them names of other organizers in the area, but you don't know those people any more and, really, you're trying to move on.

ADD MORE OF YOUR OWN STICKY SITUATIONS

CHAPTER 4: A PROCESS FOR ETHICAL DECISION-MAKING

"When counselors are faced with ethical dilemmas that are difficult to resolve, they are expected to engage in a carefully considered ethical decision-making process. Reasonable differences of opinion can and do exist among counselors with respect to the ways in which values, ethical principles, and ethical standards would be applied when they conflict. While there is no specific ethical decision-making model that is most effective, counselors are expected to be familiar with a credible model of decision making that can bear public scrutiny." — *American Counseling Association Code of Ethics (2005)*

Now we're down to brass tacks. Once you've recognized that you have an ethical problem to solve, wouldn't it be nice to have an organized way to solve it?

You do. This chapter outlines, step by step, a comprehensive process for thinking through your options, deciding what to do, and documenting the entire operation so you can show that you were conscientious in your decision if you are ever questioned about it. Portions of the process I offer here are derived from the writings of Corey, Corey, and Callanan, especially *Issues and Ethics in the Helping Professions* (2007), an excellent source of further study.

These steps should be completed in order, but you can go back and add notes to previous steps if more information comes to light as you proceed. Also, it should be emphasized that this is all "and" and no "or"—it is important that you do every step, even those you might think are unnecessary, in order to infuse your final decision with integrity.

Step 1: Prepare to Document Your Thinking

Remember algebra? You couldn't just give the answer; you had to show your work. Without seeing how you had puzzled out the problem, the teacher couldn't know if you had arrived at the right answer by luck or by logic. If you got the answer wrong, without showing your work you got neither partial credit for trying nor guidance on where you went astray.

Showing your work with an ethical problem—documenting every step of your thinking as you disentangle the issue—is important for the same reasons. In the mental health fields, client notes are official documents that could be subjected to scrutiny if the practitioner is accused of a crime or a serious ethical lapse. There are many rules and strictures about therapists' client notes, most of which are beyond our needs as organizers, but the formality of documenting an ethical decision is one rule that can guide us well.

It is highly unlikely that you will ever face review of your client notes on legal or ethical grounds, but it is possible, particularly if our industry enhances its ethical requirements someday. More salient for you now is the benefit of tracking your thinking and reviewing your notes later: Over time, you will have the chance to see yourself maturing in how you handle sticky situations, and you might even discern patterns in your client interaction that you could change to avoid recurring trouble.

Start from Scratch

The first step in making an ethical decision is opening a blank computer doc or grabbing a fresh legal pad and pen. You could also create a template or form for this, or incorporate it into your existing client notes procedures. Write linearly, in outline format, or sketch a mind map with the problem in the center and the steps radiating out in bubbles—whatever you want to do to put your own unique organizational touch to it. You don't have to write in thesis-quality sentences; a few phrases or fragments of thoughts are fine. Make it coherent enough to be understood as you complete this process and also later, if you review your notes in the future, but don't get bogged down in laboring over correct grammar, spelling, and punctuation.

Within this document, jot your notes on each of the following points. The remainder of the chapter examines these in detail:

- Identify the problem or dilemma
- Identify the potential issues involved
- Review the relevant literature and codes of ethics
- Review the applicable laws and regulations

- Obtain consultation
- Draft possible and probable courses of action
- Enumerate the consequences of each decision
- Decide on what appears to be the best course of action

When you start to tire of this process, remind yourself that you're building in integrity by being diligently comprehensive. Over time, you will derive comfort from knowing you have done important things like this carefully and completely.

Step 2: Identify the Problem or Dilemma

What exactly is wrong here? What's bothering you about the situation? What made you think it might be an ethical issue?

In this section, you're documenting your preliminary thoughts on a situation that, as of now, appears problematic. It might turn out that, after you complete this process, you realize it's not a problem at all. Great! The process is what will show you that, so it's valuable either way.

Step 3: Identify the Potential Issues Involved

Flesh out the complications and contingencies that are adding to the stickiness of the situation. Which of the key ethical tenets from Chapter 2 are involved with this situation? Are they being threatened, and how? Do they conflict with one another?

What are you afraid might happen here? What possible negative outcomes can you foresee at this point? What are the worst-case and best-case scenarios? Remember, write them all down—even the ones you think are unlikely or silly.

The notes you've made in this step and the previous one will direct your research in the next step.

Step 4: Review the Relevant Literature and Codes of Ethics

Check the NAPO and BCPO codes of ethics. Is there anything in them that speaks to this problem? Copy relevant lines into your notes in this section. Also check other, more detailed codes, such as those collected in *Codes of Ethics for the Helping Professions* (2007). Some of what is included in these codes is inapplicable to us (for example, guidance on the treatment of lab animals, or privileged communication), but overall these codes provide useful guidance for professional organizing. Copy key directives or excerpts from these codes into your notes, and be sure to include the source (e.g. "APA Code of Ethics 2005, A.2.c) to refer back to if needed. By the way, you don't have to worry about copyright when you're copying portions of a work into notes that are for your use only, not for publication or resale of any kind.

If you regularly seek guidance from a religious text, such as the Christian or Jewish Bible, the Qur'an, or the Book of Mormon, check it as well and document relevant passages. Ethics does not have to be an exclusively secular endeavor, and these texts serve as codes of ethics for the followers of their respective religions. If you are a person who is guided by religious teachings, it is important that you note this influence on your ethical decision-making, for the dual purposes of creating an accurate record of your thought process and remaining congruent with your values. However, if you are not a student or follower of a religion, don't consult its scripture: Taking snippets from a spiritual text with which you are not fully familiar fits the expression, "A little knowledge can be dangerous." Further, wrapping your argument or behavior in a cloak of false religious credibility is disrespectful at best and monstrous at worst.

Also check "the literature," an expression that refers to articles and books that address your topic directly or that cover other, similar topics in ways that allow you to extrapolate ideas relevant to your problem. In professional organizing, "the literature" includes:

- NAPO , ICD, and other official industry publications;

- the NAPO, BCPO, and ICD websites;

- NAPO and ICD conference proceedings;

- books and articles written by organizers, for organizers;

- books and articles written by organizers, for the public;

- books and articles written by non-organizers on topics of importance to organizers, including client issues and business-management issues.

You will probably fare best with materials written for organizers about client and business-management issues, because these will speak to you directly. However, if there are no such sources to be found, keep looking in the more broad-based areas until you're well into diminishing returns and you're confident that continued research won't produce anything useful. You don't have to exhaust every one of the above avenues of research, but do make a conscientious effort to find whatever guidance might be available.

If there is nothing out there, document that: "Checked *NAPO News* headlines index—nothing; checked *Chronical*s back to 2005—nothing; checked titles of NAPO conference workshops—nothing," etc.

When you do find something useful in the literature, document it with, again, phrases or short excerpts; exhaustive reproductions of the entire source are not necessary and might tire you into skimping on the parts of this process that do need to be more laborious. Be sure to include the title, author, volume, and other identifying information for each source you cite in your notes, so you or someone reviewing your notes can go back to the original if needed.

Step 5: Review the Applicable Laws and Regulations

Consider whether there are any legal ramifications here. Has something already occurred that could be construed as breaking a law or violating a local ordinance? Could laws or ordinances be violated by any future possibilities in this situation? Document your questions surrounding these points, the places you look for guidance, and any guidance you find.

In professional organizing, some areas of law that are often relevant include 1) for client work, all forms of abuse (child, domestic partner, elder, animal), financial fraud, and housing codes related to structural safety and sanitation; and 2) for peer-to-peer situations, laws governing contracts and intellectual property.

Step 6: Obtain Consultation

This is a more formal version of the phone-a-friend option on game shows like Who Wants to Be a Millionaire? The stakes are different, but the idea is the same: When you're not sure what to do, check in with someone you trust.

Obtaining consultation means seeking the advice of a peer or of a mentor, a.k.a. supervisor as explained in Chapter 2 under Boundaries of Competence In mental health, consultation is a required step when resolving an ethical dilemma.

Although media and fiction often portray therapists as arrogant know-it-alls, in truth there is a great deal of humbleness inherent to the helping professions. Practitioners with integrity recognize that they don't know everything and that, as human beings, they are always vulnerable to the influence of their personal biases and blind spots. To mitigate the risk of these human imperfections, they obtain consultation when they have decisions to make that carry important consequences for other people.

During an ethics-based consultation, make the most of your time by having all of your notes handy, including your lit review and relevant ethical codes, and be prepared to introduce the problem succinctly. Give a brief overview of the resources you have reviewed for information, and ask the consultant to point out any areas of research they can think of which you might have missed, including any laws unknown to you. Then list your choices as you see them at this point, and ask for the consultant's take on each option and also for suggestions of any options that didn't occur to you.

It is not necessary to decide during this conversation what your course of action will be. In fact, it would be premature. Remember that you will probably consult with more than one person on this and you have several more steps to work through in this decision-making model before the process will be complete. With each consultation, stay in the mindset of taking it under advisement.

Payment for Consultation

It is customary to pay for consultation time—so much so that counselors are taught to build this into their budgets. Paying for consultation legitimizes the exchange for both the consultant (the person whose guidance you seek) and the consultee (you). It makes it clear that this conversation is a business meeting, not a casual chat. The consultant has the option of declining payment, but you should always offer. For example:

Consultee (you):

"I have a dilemma and I think your input would help me. I would like to purchase an hour of your time to consult on this."

[*or, if you're not sure you can afford an entire hour:*]

"I have a dilemma and I think your input would help me. I would like to consult with you on this. What is your hourly consultation rate?" [If you can't afford a full hour, ask for a 30-minute appointment and DO NOT exceed that time.]

Consultant:

"Certainly, I'll be happy to help. My consultation rate is $$$ per hour. How about Tuesday at 10:00?"

[or]

"Certainly, I'll be happy to help, and I'll make this a pro bono hour. How about Tuesday at 10:00?" [If the consultant offers you a fee-free session, do not exceed the appointed time. If no specific end time is mentioned, limit yourself to a single call or meeting and be as efficient as possible.]

Consultation is not limited to ethical problems. You could greatly expand your expertise through occasional consultation on client strategies or business topics such as effective marketing. (In this sense it is more often referred to as coaching.) However, for ethical issues, you would be wise to think of consultation as essential.

Some professional associations eliminate budgetary constraints around seeking consultation on ethical issues by offering it as a benefit of membership. For example, the American Counseling Association has a toll-free number that members can call for free ethical consultation. Perhaps such a program could be offered by NAPO, BCPO, or ICD if enough members requested it. In the meantime, chapters could certainly fill this need for their members by implementing this as a committee or rotating volunteer position.

Who Is a "Good" Consultant?

Seek consultation with people whom you know to be ethical, measured in their thinking, and willing and able to be objective. Speak to at least one person who is skilled in or familiar with the subject matter (i.e. a peer or mentor in the industry); other people in your life, including spiritual advisors, can offer more general guidance. The stickier the problem, the more people you should consult.

Friends and relatives can be effective consultants only if the relationship will not color their thinking or cause them to be less than frank with you, and if money issues will not create awkwardness. Over time, you might develop (or you might already have) business friendships that are conducive to occasional quid pro quo consultation. In such situations, where both parties have alternated being each other's consultant and consultee, you might be able to forego paying for each other's consultation.

With business friends like these, always be careful to note when a conversation has become one of consultant/consultee rather than a discussion of routine business matters or a friendly chat. If you want to change the subject to a topic about which you want consultation, say so. This alerts the other person to pay full attention to what you are asking and to think carefully about their responses. When you are the consultant, remember that if the consultee is following the model in this chapter, what you say will become part of their documentation.

Note that these conversations need to be had in such a way that a third party could check into them later (even though it's unlikely). This means that consulting with a higher power does not fit at this step. If you indicate that you spoke to God about the matter, someone looking into it later can't go back to God and ask what was said to you. Prayer, meditation, and other forms of spiritual pondering can be documented in Step 9.

Step 7: Draft Possible Courses of Action

After you have completed the consultation step, begin listing every conceivable course of action you could take in response to this problem. Don't think about contingencies or "if/then"s at this point—just list every option. Be sure to write them all down, from the sublime to the ridiculous, because it's possible that what at first seems like a dumb idea might actually have some merit or might point you in the direction of something more credible.

Documenting all options also demonstrates everything you have considered and will ultimately show everything you rejected, including those ideas that do turn out to be ridiculous, so don't worry about looking foolish with what you record in this step. Far from silly, this exercise makes full use of your creative brainstorming ability.

Should You Make a Referral?

In our industry, this is an option that should always be considered in client situations. In mental health, referring a client to another person who does the same work you do is frowned upon unless there is a really good reason because it has a significant risk of alienating or discouraging the client. In organizing, where the work is not always so personal, this risk should still be managed, but in general, forwarding a client to another organizer is not nearly so problematic: If you handle it with sensitivity and courtesy, it is unlikely that the client will feel slighted or abandoned. Further, if another organizer is qualified to help the client in ways that you are not, it would be unethical not to make the referral.

We also often make referrals out of our industry, to people in other professions such as law, accounting, medicine, home repair, tutoring, decorating, and of course mental health. Such referrals are so frequent, and it is so common that the client needs the other person AND NOT you, not the other person AND you, that to fail to consider this type of referral as the solution to the problem might be a violation of Nonmaleficence, not to mention Boundaries of Competence.

Step 8: Enumerate the Consequences of Each Option

After you've let your creative side run free for a while, rein it in with some logic. For each of the possibilities you listed in the previous step, add what could happen if you did it. What's possible, what's probable, what's almost certain, what's very unlikely but still could happen? Be sure to note both positive and negative outcomes.

This is a great step with which to apply more of your organizational abilities. You could devise a ranking system for positive and negative consequences and score each possible course of action, effectively making your decision mathematically, or you could expand on a mind-map design to ensure you have covered all the bases. Put your skills to good use to organize the information in this section.

Step 9: Choose Your Course of Action

At this point, you have an exhaustive collection of information on which to base your final decision. You have exercised admirable due diligence in compiling research, acquiring personal guidance, and devoting introspection to the solution to this problem. Now it's time to decide what to do.

Ironically, the best way to accomplish this will often be to stop thinking about it for awhile. Switch to something different that occupies your mind and, optimally, your body too. You could try reading a really compelling mystery, working a crossword puzzle, hitting a bucket of golf balls at the driving range, bowling a few games, or challenging yourself at a skill-based, nonviolent video game. Try to find something into which you can really immerse your attention—something much more engaging than passively staring at the TV or surfing the web.

Unless you have dire time constraints, "sleep on it" for at least one night. Your subconscious is the source of creative solutions—intuitive leaps that your logical mind might block—and it can work without resistance when you sleep. Think about the problem as you're drifting off (but don't obsess to the point of insomnia), and when you wake up in the morning, pay attention to what's on your mind. It might be the answer you're seeking.

Now You Know

If the answer has become very clear, congratulations: You can now proceed with peace of mind and the confidence of your convictions, even if what you need to do is not going to be pleasant.

If no single clear answer has presented itself, you have a true ethical dilemma by Burkemper's definition: "two or more good reasons to make two or more reasonable decisions" (2002, p. 203). Review your notes again and choose a course of action. Document why you are choosing it. Ask yourself once more, "Have I honestly been diligent in seeking the best answer to this problem?" If you have, proceed with the knowledge that you have exercised the best option available to you at this time. It is entirely possible that a better option will become clear in hindsight, but it is important for you to recognize that this will not reflect poorly on your choice, if that choice was made with integrity.

Sample Application of the Process

Here is an example of what this chapter's decision-making process might look like, using the case described earlier of the elderly woman living in a high-fire-risk home.

Step 1: Prepare to Document

—starting with pad and paper; might add a mind map later

Step 2: ID the Problem

—elderly woman, lives alone, able to care for herself, but hoards newspapers and a smoker—multiple stacks in every room, some to the ceiling, house is a firetrap—concerned for her safety and that of neighbors, possibly rescue workers, but don't want to threaten her independence (autonomy)

<u>Step 3: ID Potential Issues</u>

—she is in danger but won't admit it

—can care for herself in every other way, so still entitled to autonomy?

—balancing risk to her vs. risk to community and other people—whose rights are more important?

<u>Step 4: Lit and Codes Review</u>

—client dignity and welfare are utmost (ACA)—would taking this choice away from her violate dignity? Well, she's living in squalor right now, which isn't dignified...and it's a threat to her welfare

—duty to warn—clients who are danger to themselves—this applies to counselors when clients express suicidality and homicidality; nothing clearly about self-neglect, plus she's oriented to place, time, identity, etc., so no grounds for calling her incompetent—looks to me like autonomy and informed consent would trump the potential danger here

—also duty to warn neighbors and rescue personnel....

—NAPO code doesn't address this—says have to maintain confidentiality, but doesn't address breaching it for client safety—same with BCPO

—tons of media reports of people who hoard dying trapped in the hoard

—reviewed ICD Clutter-Hoarding Scale and notes from Kristin Bergfeld's presentation on hoarding from last conference—this house is severe—Level IV or V on C-H Scale

Step 5: Legal Review

—on city ordinance website, no hits on "squalor" or "hoard"

—skimmed sections of city Code of Ordinance: Part 14: Building and Housing Code (nothing pertinent to excess materials in a house) and Part 16: Fire Prevention Code (nothing); also General Offenses Code Chapter 660: Offenses Relating to Property (nothing re: indiv homeowners) and Chapter 676: Safety, Sanitation and Health (seems like it's all about public property).

—676.04 disallows anything that causes an offensive odor, but you can't smell her house from outside.

—a ha—Part 14 Title 6 Misc Building Regs: allows the city to order a person to vacate premises if deemed hazardous; also allows for order for abatement but specifies plumbing, structural damage etc, nothing about contents—could probably be lumped under "premises"—so, yes, the city could force a cleanup or eviction

Step 6: Consultation

—talked to Jane Eldercare, PO specializing in senior downsizing—she agreed it is unsafe and that she would be inclined to contact the city if the client can't be persuaded—suggested calling the city to ask their procedure before revealing the client's name/address

—talked to Bob Lawyerman, estate attorney—suggested conservatorship, where someone becomes the guardian of her finances—if she has any assets, a conservator could hire a clean-up crew on her behalf and someone to come out every couple weeks to check on her and dismantle any new hoarding

—talked to Dr. Helper, local psychologist—she agreed that forcibly abating the hoard would be traumatic and the client would likely rebuild it; at her age, could also trigger a decline in cognitive acuity; offered to come out and talk to the client, perform a mini-assessment onsite, and give further recommendations—need client to sign dr's consent form for this

Step 7: Draft Possible Actions

1. do nothing

2. call the city and report her

3. call the city and ask about their procedure anonymously—not giving my name or hers

4. call the city and give my name but not hers, ask what they would do in this situation

5. call the city and county and ask if there are any resources for hoarding abatement, elderly mental health care or social services; then call those agencies and ask how they would handle it

6. try to persuade her on my own that it's unsafe, get her to let go of some things

7. try to persuade her to talk to the doctor; get her to sign the consent form

8. if she refuses to talk to the doctor, forge her name on the consent form to get the doctor out to the house

9. call an insurance agent?

10. ask her again if she has any family and try to find them? suggest conservatorship to them?

11. talk to her next-door neighbors—maybe they know something's wrong, warn them if not, ask them not to report her because I'm working on it—see if they know of any family, and also suggest that they plan on warning any rescue personnel who come to the home if there is an emergency

12. sneak in at night and take the papers little by little

13. offer to take her somewhere she wants to go, then instead take her to a nursing home or hospital and tell them she's a danger to herself

14. team up with the neighbors and just take the papers—she wouldn't be strong enough to stop us

Step 8: Consequences

1. do nothing: can't—why bother with all of this? could this even be nonmaleficence? -NO

2. report her to city: then I would lose any control over situation, might not be able to help or make it easier on her; but would also be anonymous so she wouldn't blame me -NO

3. ask city anon: they'd probably give me vague info, couldn't be sure it would be accurate, honest -NO

4. call the city w/my name but not hers: might be more honest; might buy me some time to negotiate a deal for her -MAYBE

5. call the city & county re: resources: yes, should do this regardless—they might have an agency that handles this, and as social services people, maybe they would be more compassionate—actually help her to choose to change rather than forcing her -YES

6. keep trying to get her to let go: did this already, didn't work; I'm not a counselor, so it could be risky for her -NO

7. persuade to talk to Dr: yes, I could do this—if she agrees, it would put her in contact with a person who is qualified to help -MAYBE

8. forge her name on consent: the doctor would no longer trust me, neither would the client; if I'm going to have to resort to deception, break fidelity, should at least not betray other helpers -NO

9. ins agent?: Not sure what I would ask or say... don't know if she has insurance or with which co. -NO

10. ask her again re: family: could try this—might make her suspicious or agitated, though—if I only get one shot at getting her to agree to something, it should be the doctor -MAYBE

11. ask neighbors re: family: could try this; it violates her confidentiality, but it protects them from harm (justice) which to me is the more important of the two; if it goes to an abatement, family would be helpful -MAYBE

also re: have them warn rescue personnel in meantime (beneficence, justice): -YES!

12. sneak in & take papers: might make her think she's going crazy; as Dr. said, could actually make her lose her grip on reality (could be actual maleficence—doing harm); plus illegal—stealing, even if the property has no monetary value -NO

13. trick her into going to hosp: really extreme—only as a very last resort—she would never trust me again, and chances are they wouldn't keep her forever, so then she'd be back in the house and I would have no clout with her (fidelity) -NO

14. take papers with neighbors: even worse than 12 -NO

Step 9: Choose

Do #5—call city and county, talk to whoever services residents with this problem. If that pans out, work with them to help her. If not, do 7—Dr consent (and 10, ask about family, if she's not agitated, after she signs consent) and also 11—talk to neighbors. Work with Dr from there to figure out what to do next.

✧

That's the end of the sample application of the ethical decision-making process. Did you notice that it's not perfect? What you see here is unrevised, unedited—I role-played how I would work the process for this dilemma using the actual codes of my city for the legal review, drew on some actual past consultation for Step 6, and left the whole thing in first-draft form for you, dear reader. It contains redundancies, abbreviations, some dumb ideas—and that's how it should be. The key tracking of the thought process is there, and that's all that matters. To take more time to make it pretty would be over-organizing.

If you work the process for this same problem, you'll come up with some different ideas. (No need to send them to me— this scenario is fictitious.) Even if you arrived at the same final answer, the "show your work" portion of the process would be different, especially your lit and legal reviews and your consultation. This is why thinking it through this way is so important—it gives you the best chance of being comprehensive, arriving at a defensible choice, and retaining the evidence of how you got there.

CHAPTER 5: HIGH NOON: CONFRONTING A SUSPECTED ETHICAL VIOLATOR

Perhaps the most uncomfortable part of taking the ethical high road is the prospect of bringing up a problem with another person. Sometimes it's a client whom you need to persuade or inform in some way that they're not going to like. Sometimes it's declining to do something and in the process causing disappointment, hurt feelings, or even anger. Sometimes it's admitting you've made a mistake. These scenarios are awkward enough, even when there was no malice involved on either side.

The stickiest of all sticky situations happens when you catch a peer behaving unethically. It can feel like the weight of the world is on your shoulders when you realize that you now have an ethical obligation to address the situation in some way. It could be very tempting to just let it go. As with every other ethical decision, it's all a matter of context, circumstances, the particular situation, and so on, so it's possible that doing nothing might be a viable option (for example, if you think it could put you in danger), but only you can know that. Bottom line, you have to decide what's right. Here are some ideas to help you through this storm.

Chapter 5

Do My Eyes Deceive Me?

Be very sure about how you're interpreting the situation. Is it really what it looks like? If you are inclined to think there are always one right way and a bunch of wrong ways to do something, be cautious here: It might be that the other person's way is acceptable, even if it's not what you would do.

For another way to check yourself on this, recall the distinction between boundary crossings and boundary violations. Which does this situation seem to be? Remember that this question is largely a matter of your interpretation since we have no master list of small and large offenses to refer to.

Speak Softly and Carry a Big Bucket of Tact

If at this point you're still concerned that it's an actual boundary violation, or that it's a boundary crossing but the colleague doesn't seem to have full control of the situation, it's time to speak to the person.

President Teddy Roosevelt famously said, "Speak softly and carry a big stick"—in other words, give the person a diplomatic fair warning before you pummel them with consequences. At this point in our problem, it's not yet time for the "big stick": For one thing, you don't yet know if there is a violation, and for another thing, since our industry's codes of ethics are largely unenforced, you probably have no stick to wield anyway. Any progress you can make will have to come from the "speak softly" part—your ability to inform, express concern, and encourage a higher level of behavior without provoking defensiveness.

Yes, that's a tall order. Before you let it intimidate you, though, remember that most ethical violations happen inadvertently or out of ignorance. It is unlikely that the person wants to be unethical (although not unprecedented). If you approach the conversation with the intention of helping a well-meaning colleague to avoid embarrassment (think toilet paper on the shoe), it will be easier to find the courage to do it and you will be less likely to come across as accusatory or judgmental.

Finding the Words

The moment of truth has arrived. You and your colleague are in the same room and the colleague is not talking to anyone right now. You can just walk over and ask if they have a minute. No one else is nearby. Time to make your move. But what will you actually say once you have the person's attention? Aim for a spirit of camaraderie rather than division; if broaching this subject is really hard for you to do, say so. Use humor if it's natural for you to downplay the tension. Here are some ideas:

I'm wondering about something that has to do with you.

I heard something the other day that I thought you might want to know about.

I'm nervous about bringing this up, but I'm afraid it could harm you if I don't.

This is awkward for me. I want to ask you about something I've noticed and I'm hoping you won't mind helping me to interpret it.

We've known each other a long time now, so I'm sure this will be okay to say, but I'm still a little nervous.

I'm troubled by something I heard you say last week, and since I respect you, this is me trying to have the guts to tell you about it.

I have something to ask you and I really wish I had a couple glasses of wine, but here goes nuthin'.

I've been reading this ethics book, and I have a dilemma that I hope you can help me with.

We don't know each other very well yet, so I hope you won't mind me bringing this up.

I'd like to check in with you on something I'm confused about.

I've got this situation, and the way it looks doesn't fit my impression of you. Can we talk about it?

Notice that most of these suggestions start with "I" or "We" and none of them starts with "You." This is intentional: It sends the message that "we're in this together and I'm not attacking you." For this to come across as genuine, though, you have to actually mean it. Remind yourself as you're approaching the person that your purpose is to help a colleague, not to collect a scalp.

Once you get past your opening lines, relay the situation as objectively as possible: "You gave out photocopies of an ICD publication," not "You violated ICD's copyright." Make your statement in a way that shows you're considering the possibility that there was no ethical lapse.

Then relay your ethical concern in the form of a questioning statement: "I'm wondering if you realized those are copyrighted," or "I'm wondering if you asked their permission to distribute them." Can you hear how this is even less confrontational than, "Do you realize those are copyrighted?" or "Did you get their permission?" The "I'm wondering" statement lets the other person know you have a question, but it doesn't exactly demand an answer. It gives the other person a chance to clarify without being abruptly put on the spot.

Here's another piece of advice from the counseling world: When you're confronting (and that's what you're doing, albeit very gently), avoid the word "why." It is very difficult to say that word without sounding judgmental, even if you bury it in the "I'm wondering" construction. So instead of "I'm wondering why you did that," try "I'm wondering how come you did that" or "I'm wondering what led you to that choice." It's clunky grammar, but much less aggressive.

Dropping the E-Bomb

It's possible that your well-intentioned overture won't be at all well-received, no matter how diplomatically you present it. The person might still get defensive and snap at you. If you have the, er, ovaries to continue the conversation, here are some valid responses to ugly retorts:

This is none of your business!

> Sure it is. It came to my attention and that makes it my business.*

How dare you question my integrity?

> I'm trying to help you SHOW your integrity. What you did looks ambiguous, and I'm trying to help you clarify.*

You have no right to question me.

> Sure I do. In fact, it's my ethical obligation.*

Are you calling me [a liar / a cheat / dishonest / whatever]?

> Not at all. I'm letting you know how this looks and I'm offering you the chance to fix it.*

*After each of these, quickly, add this:

> I believe you intended to do the right thing but it didn't come across that way. I thought you would

want to know. I would hate to think you want to be UNETHICAL.

There. You dropped the E-bomb. That will either snap the person into realizing this is serious, or it will provoke a bigger tantrum. If the former, perhaps now you'll be able to have a grown-up conversation about it. Take a deep breath, switch back to your original approach, and try to get your message across.

If the latter—if the person launches into a fit of epic proportions, or what my grandmother called a hemorrhage of green paint—disengage. Nothing good can come from more dialogue now.

It Really Was a Violation. What Now?

The best-case scenario: The conversation went well. You managed to say what you needed to, and the other person listened and realized that they had made an ethical lapse. They promised to make amends. Now what should you do?

First, keep it between the two of you. Give them a chance to correct it if the situation can be corrected (for example, sending a letter to the ICD acknowledging the mistake with a check for the copies of the publication). If it's a mistake of the "live, learn, and don't do it again" variety, give the person the benefit of the doubt and expect that they have grown from this experience. It might even turn out that by extending yourself to help this person, you have earned a new degree of respect from them plus the opportunity to work together or to ask for their support for a future effort of your own.

What if it didn't go quite that well? What if the person said they would make amends, but hasn't, or worse, what if the conversation descended into defensive denial or a thuggish "what're YOU gonna do about it"?

If you are convinced, really convinced, that this person did something unethical, knows it, and has no intention of changing, now is the time you'll wish you had that big stick. Instead, you have only one certain option and two other outside possibilities, none of which is likely to be especially gratifying:

Shunning. Distance yourself professionally from the other person. Decline to be associated with them in any way, including committee work and client referrals. Be very careful never to be seen having an informal conversation with such a person: Chances are you're not the only one who has recognized their questionable ethics, and you don't want your reputation to be tarnished through association. However, at the same time, be careful what you say by way of explanation to third parties. You don't want to be accused of slander. If pressed, do what divorcing celebrities do: blame it on "irreconcilable differences" and let people draw their own inferences.

Legal action. In rare cases where an ethical breach is also illegal, you have the option of consulting with an attorney or the police to look into the matter. This would be a legitimate response if, for example, a new organizer in your area appropriated your company name and slogan. Of course, just because it's justifiable doesn't mean it will be affordable, as you can imagine if you guess at the number of attorney hours this could take to resolve, or fruitful, as you know if you've ever tried to collect on a monetary judgment against a regular person with regular-sized assets (or worse, a crook who already blew it all).

BCPO or ICD complaint. There are currently two narrow routes for requesting ethical accountability in professional organizing. If the violator has earned the Certified Professional Organizer (CPO®) credential from the Board of Certification for Professional Organizers, or BCPO, that means they agreed to abide by the BCPO Code of Ethics and to be held accountable for compliance. Any person, not just another CPO®, can bring an ethical complaint about a CPO® or prospective CPO® to the BCPO. If the person is an ICD member (technically they are called subscribers) and has misrepresented their ICD credentials, only another ICD subscriber can bring a complaint to the ICD for investigation.

Perhaps in the future, professional organizing will establish codes of ethics that are enforceable for everyone, not just the credentialed minority. Until then, these options are the closest we can come to Roosevelt's big-stick diplomacy.

As tempting as it may be, resist the urge to retaliate with questionable behavior of your own. That would just undermine your own ethics. Remember that wise (but frustrating) advice from your childhood for dealing with mean kids: Don't stoop to their level.

CONCLUSION: IT'S A GRAY WORLD

If you didn't believe this before, I hope you do now: There is no secret catalog of right answers out there. Ethics at the end of this book is just as gray as it was on the first page. However, we have managed to force some order onto it, and it's not a false front: It is possible to dip into the swirling morass and make good decisions by working systematically. As professional organizers, we do it every day with objects, data, and time management. With ethics, we've found yet another problem to which organization is the solution.

But is it really that simple? Follow the formula and you'll arrive at the ethical thing to do? Picture Adolf Hitler working this model and a gaping loophole appears—one that, with people other than genocidal despots, is filled by individual character.

If you're an irredeemable jerk, this process isn't going to turn you good. You will either find a way to skew the moral principles to support you (Hitler worked the Justice and Fidelity angles and bewitched millions of people) or you'll play in the gray to cleverly justify your actions (I berate my clients to motivate them; I pad my billable hours because my kids need braces; the lies I tell are little and white). There is one more key ethical ingredient that we haven't yet mentioned, and it plays a big part in character development. It's your conscience.

Most (but not all) people have one. If you are able to empathize with your clients' pain, meaning you know what it feels like to hurt as they do, and if you're motivated to prevent other people from hurting (we usually refer to this as helping, but just as often it's the prevention of harm), and if you're willing to sometimes even inconvenience yourself in the service of this goal (perhaps by speaking up when you suspect an ethical violation), you have a conscience. With this all-important piece of human software and a strong foundation in ethical teachings, you are relatively unlikely to cause harm, even inadvertently.

In other words, if your heart's in the right place, you're systematically thinking through your actions, and you have the intestinal fortitude to do the right thing once you've discovered it, you have as much control over ethics as it's possible to have. So relax, and trust that when the big gray world brings you an ethical dilemma, you'll be able to figure it out.

REFERENCES AND FURTHER READING

The articles below should be available in larger university libraries; look for the books on Amazon.com, Half.com, or the authors' websites.

American Counseling Association. (2005). Code of ethics. In *Codes of Ethics for the Helping Professions* (3rd ed., pp. 9-35). Belmont, CA: Thomson Brooks/Cole, 2007.

    See book reference below.

Board of Certification for Professional Organizers. (2019). *Code of ethics.* Dunedin, FL: Author.

    Available at

    http://www.certifiedprofessionalorganizers.org/ COE.html

Burkemper, E. M. (2002). Family therapists' ethical decision-making processes in two duty-to-warn situations. *Journal of Marital and Family Therapy, 28*(2), 203-211.

    Source of the definition of an ethical dilemma used in this book.

Chicago Manual of Style, 15th ed. (2003). Chicago and London: University of Chicago Press.

    Authoritative source for guidance on copyright and fair use. See Rights and Permissions section. Some portions also available at http://www.chicagomanualofstyle.org

Codes of Ethics for the Helping Professions. (2007). (3rd ed.). Belmont, CA: Thomson Brooks/Cole.

    Contains the official codes of ethics of: American Association for Marriage and Family Therapy; American Counseling Association; American Mental Health Counselors Association; American Psychological Association; American School Counselor Association; Association for Counselor Education and Supervision; Association for Specialists in Group Work; Canadian Counselling Association; Canadian Psychological Association; Commission on Rehabilitation Counselor Certification; International Association of Marriage and

Family Counselors; National Association of Social Workers; National Board for Certified Counselors; National Organization for Human Service Education.

Corey, G., Corey, M. S., & Callanan, P. (2007). *Issues and ethics in the helping professions* (7th ed.). Pacific Grove, CA: Brooks/Cole.

A textbook for counseling students that includes self-assessments to determine one's attitudes and beliefs about ethical issues, a step-by-step process for ethical decision-making, and guidance on dealing with unethical colleagues.

Cottone, R. R., & Claus, R. E. (2000). Ethical decision-making models: A review of the literature. *Journal of Counseling & Development, 78*(3), 275-283.

Covey, Stephen R. (1989). *The Seven Habits of Highly Effective People.* New York: Simon & Schuster.

Hansen, N. D., & Goldberg, S. G. (1999). Navigating the nuances: A matrix of considerations for ethical-legal dilemmas. *Professional Psychology: Research and Practice, 30*(5), 495-503.

Herlihy, B., & Corey, G. (2006). *ACA Ethical Standards Casebook* (6th ed.). Alexandria, VA: American Counseling Association.

Written by two respected experts on counseling ethics; gives detailed analysis of the American Counseling Association's Code of Ethics and includes many case studies and quizzes.

Hill, M., Glaser, K., & Harden, J. (1995). A feminist model for ethical decision making. In E. J. Rave & C. C. Larson (Eds.), *Ethical decision making in therapy: Feminist perspectives* (pp. 18-37). New York: Guilford.

Institute for Challenging Disorganization. (2018). *Code of ethics.* Larchmont, NY: Author.

Available at https://www.challengingdisorganization.org/code-of-ethics

Jordan, A. E., & Meara, N. M. (1990). Ethics and the professional practice of psychologists: The role of virtues and principles. *Professional Psychology: Research and Practice, 21*(2), 107-114.

Kenyon, P. (1999). *What would you do?: An ethical case workbook for human service professionals.* Pacific Grove, CA: Brooks/Cole Publishing.

National Association of Productivity and Organizing Professionals. (2015). *Code of ethics.* Mount Laurel, NJ: Author.
> Available at https://www.napo.net/page/about_ethics

National Study Group on Chronic Disorganization. (2003). The NSGCD Clutter Hoarding Scale (No. 006). St. Louis, MO: Author.
> Original name of ICD Clutter-Hoarding Scale published by the Institute for Challenging Disorganization. Available at https://www.challengingdisorganization.org/clutter-hoarding-scale-

Neukrug, E., Lovell, C., & Parker, R. J. (1996). Employing ethical codes and decision-making models: A developmental process. *Counseling and Values, 40*(2), 98-106.

Stadler, H. A. (1996). Making hard choices: Clarifying controversial ethical issues. *Counseling and Human Development, 19,* 1-10.

Sgro, V. (2003). Walking your talk: Ethics and the professional organizer. *NAPO News* (May-June), 12.
> Explanation of NAPO's code of ethics. [Out of print]

U.S. Copyright Office. www.copyright.gov
> Information on intellectual property rights.

INDEX

9

9/11 · 13

A

abuse · 34, 41, 66
ACA · *See* American Counseling Association
accountability · 32, 91
ADHD · *See* attention deficit/hyperactivity disorder
advertising · *See* marketing
age · 16, 77
American Counseling Association · 3, 59, 69, 75, 95, 96
animals · 43, 63
attention deficit/hyperactivity disorder · 45, *See also* chronic disorganization
attribution · 28, 29, 30, 31, *See also* intellectual property
autonomy, moral principle of · 9, 11, 75

B

backsliding · 9
bartering · 33, 47, *See also* compensation, manner of
BCPO · *See* Board of Certification for Professional Organizers
beneficence, moral principle of · 9, 11, 15, 80
bias · 17, 18, 33, 42, 66
big-stick diplomacy · 84, 90, 91
Board of Certification for Professional Organizers · 2, 3, 28, 63, 64, 69, 75, 91, 95
boundaries of behavior · 2
boundaries of competence, ethical tenet of · 2, 18, 19, 20, 21, 66, 72
boundary crossing · 12, 21, 23, 27, 84
boundary violation · 12, 13, 21, 27, 84
brainstorming · 4, 71
bullying · 9

www.ingramcontent.com/pod-product-compliance
Lightning Source LLC
Chambersburg PA
CBHW060055100426
42742CB00014B/2836